LEARNING CENTERS AND INDIVIDUALIZED READING
In Behavioral Terms

By
Alex W. Vlangas
Richard J. Williams
Towson State College

MSS Information Corporation
655 Madison Avenue, New York, N.Y. 10021

Library of Congress Cataloging in Publication Data

Vlangas, Alex W
    Learning centers and individualized reading --
in behavioral terms.

    1. Reading. 2. Individualized reading in-
struction. I. Williams, Richard Jay, 1928-
joint author. II. Title. [DNLM: 1. Learning.
2. Reading. LB1573 V866L 1973]
LB1050.V55 1973   372.4'147   72-13937
ISBN 0-8422-0292-7

To Cia and Ruth

TABLE OF CONTENTS

CHAPTER I

PREFACE

On college campuses and in public schools throughout the country much is being taught and discussed in three areas relating to reading instruction: individualizing instruction, utilizing learning centers, and stating objectives in behavioral terms.

The authors of this text with a wealth of experience in public education and long-standing involvement in the training of teachers, both experienced and inexperienced, are attempting to provide some "down to earth" information on the above topics that will help teachers "new" and "old" to be able to individualize learnings in their classrooms.

CHAPTER II

PHILOSOPHY OF INDIVIDUALIZED INSTRUCTION

General

The goal of helping each individual to achieve his unique character is one that has its roots in the ideas of the early philosophers. This goal has always been one of gigantic proportions and seems to grow greater each passing year. As life becomes more complex, the need for uniqueness and independence seems more and more to be needed and less and less able to be obtained. It is the schools of this country which must assume the awesome burden and privilege for preserving and developing the special abilities and character of each individual student.

The foundations of our nation clearly show evidence of a commitment to the individual human being. As the decades passed, the Common School grew with an increasing dedication to developing the unique personal powers of the individual. As cultural patterns and pressures changed, schools veered more and more to mass groupings, mass curriculums and mass organizational patterns. A justified emphasis on group values and the ability to live well in groups seems a necessity yet this does not lessen the need for individuality.

Taking care of individual differences has been seen and discussed as desirable for nearly all of the decades of the

Twentieth Century. Educators have tried to devise ways to provide for ranges of achievement, competence, and interest. Lately the concept has broadened to include learning styles, and the development of the inner person - his special personality, character, and style.

Good administrators and teachers try to devise systems to accomodate differences and to develop creative, unique persons. Today there is more emphasis upon programmed learning, tutorials, independent study, learning centers, contracts, individualized learning kits, media centers, and other individualized approaches to reading and to learning. It must be remembered, however, that no programmed book, no special project nor any machine will accomplish what is needed in reading. The teacher of reading is the major key. Only as the teacher provides the climate of openness, stimulates the learner, and surrounds the learner with a challenging set of learning tools will the individual have the possibility of counteracting the standardizing influences in schools and in society today.

Schools and society are geared to working with people in groups. To be sure we sometimes get to work in a one-to-one relationship but schools can and should seek out more ways of dealing with individuals.

A vast part of what is done in schools toward developing individuals has minimal potential if aspects of community life negate it. The same is true of the climate of leadership surrounding the schools. The professional and lay leaders determine how wide or how circumscribed the horizons of teachers and students will be. These leaders must allow doors to open, imagination to be released, and special aptitudes, differences, and qualities to flourish.

The school and the community as part of society must be interested in fostering individual differences and individualized learning. These groups must conduct themselves in a certain way. They must ask questions and provide answers to questions relating to physical facilities, to school organizational patterns, to the types and styles of teachers and teaching, to the curriculum, and to instructional methods and materials. In addition, regulations relating to education of state and Federal governments may need to be examined and the social setting, the parents, and the Board of Education in the local community must be a crucial consideration as they play a significant role if the school is to encourage the strengths of individualized teaching and learning.

If our society then supports a concern for the individual spirit and for the allied idea of individualized learning, we must continue to move toward a practical methodology which may appeal to individual children and foster independence of thinking and of operation in the classroom and hopefully in other segments of society outside of school.

Learning Centers

Learning Centers may be a small breakthrough toward a more open, individualized way to implement learning to read in a classroom and school setting. The Learning Center in its fullest interpretation implies an expanded learning environment, fuller and freer choices for the learner, greater independence on the part of the participant, and revised arrangements and goals for the classroom, school, and community. The child should be helped to grow in his own style, at his own speed, and, most importantly, in uniqueness.

CHAPTER III

DEFINITION AND DESCRIPTION OF BEHAVIORAL OBJECTIVES

Significance of Behavioral Objectives

In educational circles today there are three terms being used quite frequently. They are: instructional goals, educational objectives, and behavioral objectives. What they mean is objectives in education which are stated in behavioral terms. For the purpose of this text the term behavioral objective will be used because it seems to say what it means.

If a teacher is to be effective in his instruction he must first decide what his purpose is and then select a procedure or method which will help him fulfill such a purpose. This thinking is not new because for years teachers have been specifying goals or purposes for their educational endeavors. The problem has been that such goals have been too ambiguous, vague, and non-measurable. By defining objectives in behavioral terms the ambiguity, vagueness and non-measurability can be eliminated.

Identification of Behavioral Objectives

To help identify such objectives look at the ten items below and see if you can decide which objectives are stated in behavioral terms and which are not. On a piece of paper write the numbers one to ten and next to each write yes, if you feel the objective is stated in behavioral terms, and no if you think it is not stated in behavioral terms.

13

1. To be able to understand the principles of good reading instruction

2. To be able to list three reading approaches

3. To be able to know how to really teach reading

4. To be able to match the first ten capital and lower case letters

5. To be able to say orally at least eight of twelve sight words

6. To be able to select two descriptive words in a paragraph

7. To really appreciate reading for enjoyment

8. To be able to distinguish between fact and opinion

9. To be able to enjoy poetry

10. To grasp the significance of the theme of a story

The behavioral objective of the writers of this text is for the reader to be able to identify all of them by answering yes or no as to which objective above is behavioral and which objective is non-behavioral before finishing the reading of this section of the book.

In order for an objective to be meaningfully stated it must convey to all readers the intent of the writer. There are certain words which lend themselves to being precise and others which are less precise. If the writer uses precise words he should be able to state his objectives in a way which every reader will comprehend. Examples of such words are:

Precise Words	Less Precise Words
to identify	to perceive
to list	to know
to point to	to appreciate
to name	to grasp the signifi-
to order	cance of
to demonstrate	to enjoy
to describe	to understand
to write	to really appreciate
to recite	to really enjoy
to underline	to learn
to mark	to believe

It becomes obvious then that behavioral objectives must be defined in terms of specific behaviors accepting that behavior is any activity which is visible as displayed by the learner. This behavior can be seen and measured by the teacher. By using words which are more precise, by their own nature, such behaviors can be more easily identified. To learn, to know, or to really enjoy may mean one thing to the writer and another thing to the reader. Whereas, to name, to point, or to list, will more than likely mean the same thing to the student as it does to the teacher.

There are three other considerations in using behavioral objectives. They are the conditions under which the behaviors are demonstrated, the minimal expectations for the individual, and the minimal expectations of the group or class. The first consideration in relation to this text is that each behavioral objective will be defined for each learning station constructed. The minimal level of expectation for each student and each group will have to be ascertained by the teacher using the learning station. The teacher may determine for instance, that each student working with a learning station should get 80% of the items in that station correct while another teacher using the same learning station might feel each student should get 95% of the items correct. It might very well be the same in terms of the minimal group level. One teacher could possibly set the standard that 75% of the group should get 80% of the items correct while another teacher might set the standard that 80% of the group should get 90% of the items correct.

In using behavioral objectives to construct learning stations there are a number of advantages which include:

1. Focusing on the learner

2. Seeing precise relationships

3. Gearing instruction toward capabilities of the student

4. Increasing motivation of students

5. Expecting students to be successful

6. Helping students feel more secure

7. Pin-pointing specific learning skills

8. Involving students to see where they are going

9. Sequencing of skills so that one can build on the other

10. Permitting better evaluation

Return now to the ten items mentioned earlier as good or not-so-good behavioral objectives and see if the reader would change any of them. The answers should be as follows:

1. No	6. Yes
2. Yes	7. No
3. No	8. Yes
4. Yes	9. No
5. Yes	10. No

If the reader sees that he is not proficient by now in being able to identify a behavioral objective he may wish to read one or both of the following texts:

Mager, Robert. Preparing Instructional Objectives, Fearon Publishers, 1962.

Popham, James. Establishing Instructional Goals, Prentice-Hall Inc., 1970.

CHAPTER IV

DEFINITION AND DESCRIPTION
OF LEARNING CENTERS

Introduction

One of the major goals of elementary schools today is individualizing instruction to develop independence, to foster greater self-motivation, and to personalize learnings.

Individualizing learning and teaching through learning centers and stations is an alternative to the concept of seatwork with children seated at desks working on ditto sheets or copying work from the chalkboard. Learning centers allow for more freedom of movement and freedom of choices for children. Children are allowed to make some choices of the activities which they will do each day. They are trained, also, to assume responsibilities for completing their work and, more importantly, to check their own progress. This checking allows for immediate reinforcement and for evaluation of one's own growth.

Definitions

Learning Center--A learning center is usually a designated area to which a child or a few children go to have a total learning experience. This center may consist of one independent activity or of several sequential or related activities through which the student works in order to develop a skill, to apply a skill, or to develop a concept.

Learning station--A learning station is one segment of a learning center which stresses one skill, concept or interest.

18

Criteria for Developing Centers

In order to clarify the definitions as stated above a description of a learning center and a learning station might help. A meaningful learning center should have as its outcome a measurable change of behavior and include:

1. Stations having clear purposes stated in the form of behavioral objectives

2. Directions for stations which are simple and clear enough for each participant to understand

3. Stations having high interest appeal for the participant

4. Stations which are easy to evaluate by the participants

5. Stations which meet the individual abilities of the participant

6. A variety of stations presenting skills, interests or concepts meaningful and hopefully enjoyable to the participants

7. Stations which are creative and appealing

8. Some stations with open-ended options where children may pursue their own interests.

Types of Centers

Traditionally, good teachers have had interest centers in their classrooms. Science corners, reading corners, library tables, and free-time areas have been provided. These centers are still approved and useful as they allow for some of the open-ended learnings that children should be allowed and encouraged to pursue. However, the methods and materials used by these teachers, in many cases, were not clear and precise and as a result boys and girls were merely exposed to an interest area and hopefully something would happen. Hopefully, stating a goal for an interest center will give the center clear direction and purpose.

In addition, there are skill-development learning centers which if skillfully prepared by the teacher allow for several levels of skill development in sequential order.

The third type of center may be called a concept center. Skillfully designed a group may be guided through the various steps required to grasp the concept, for instance, of the differences between fact and opinion.

As just mentioned, learning centers are either skill-centered, interest-centered or concept-centered and should contain many of the structural elements presented in the previous list of what good learning centers include.

Implementation of Learning Centers

A Climate for Centers

The climate for the fruitful use of learning centers no matter what the physical organization of the school must come from a combination of factors. These include an open, aware, and supportive administration, an enlightened and hard-working teaching staff, an understanding community, and a willing and increasingly independent student body.

The introduction of the learning center concept must be a measured, gradual process both in the classroom or learning area and in the school. Children must be introduced to the concept in a carefully planned manner so that their independence and responsibility may be given time to grow. A proposed plan for introducing learning centers in a classroom or in a learning module might proceed as follows:

1. A few learning centers are available to students before school either for the whole class or for a small group.

2. A few learning centers are available to students during free time either for the whole class or for a small group.

3. One reading group is instructed in the use of learning centers and is allowed to work in centers while the teacher instructs the remaining children. Each group in turn is trained and gets a turn.

4. Several hours a week are designated for learning centers and all children participate at that time.

5. An extended block of time is devoted to a subject or to related subjects. For example, the majority of the learning experiences in the language arts may be taught, reviewed, and evaluated through learning center activities. Therefore, the whole morning segment of time could be spent in spelling, reading, creative writing, and handwriting experiences.

6. Virtually the whole day is devoted to teaching and learning in learning centers. Centers are used in all subjects with the group getting together daily for starting assignments, introducing reading stories, meeting new concepts, and planning for future activities.

Criteria for Learning Centers

1. Learning centers should serve as a good model for children. They should:
   a. be attractive
   b. have objectives which are behaviorally stated

21

c. have clear directions
d. be written in language which children can read
e. be grammatically correct
f. be self-checking

2. Learning centers may serve as an activity for one day, for several days, or for a week or longer. They are equally useful for teaching, for review, or for reteaching.

3. Learning centers should be evaluated regularly and carefully. Teachers should ask themselves whether the centers engender sustained interest and growth in students.

School Design and Learning Centers

Using learning centers should be a flexible concept whether arranged in a self-contained classroom by one teacher or arranged to serve a team or module in an open-space school. In the self-contained classroom, learning centers need not be contained by walls but can overflow into halls, storage rooms, and into classrooms of other teachers who are developing similar concepts or units.

Open Space Schools

The greater the flexibility in school plant and school design the easier it is to set up learning stations within learning centers. This does not mean, however, that Learning Centers cannot be used effectively in a traditional or "egg crate" type school.

In a totally "open space" school or in schools designed for team teaching where there are open space modules, teachers can designate areas and set up learning stations which can be used cooperatively by one or more teachers. The main advantage in this type of school plant is that students are in

22

the view of both teachers at all times. The diagram below illustrates one type of open space organization.

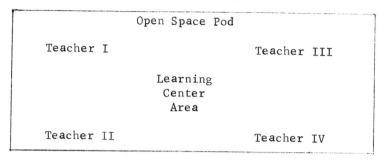

It can be seen from this diagram that four teachers might cooperatively set up learning centers which children from all four classes could use and still be in the view of each teacher.

In a school which has operable, collapsable or no walls between two classrooms the learning centers might be set up as illustrated in the following diagram:

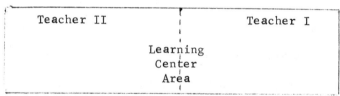

Such an organization as illustrated above shows the same advantages as an open space module except that two teachers can work cooperatively in setting up the learning center areas instead of four.

Traditional Schools

If a school is arranged on a self-contained classroom design and it is an "egg crate" school where each teacher has a room and a certain number of pupils within that room for which he is responsible, there are a number of ways that teachers can organize physically for learning centers. Some illustrations are:

Room I	Room II	Room III
Teacher	Learning	Teacher
Students	Centers	Students

Two or more teachers could work cooperatively and use a separate room to set up learning centers. The disadvantage in this organization would be that the students would be out of the teachers view when using such centers. An instructional aide, a student teacher or even a parent could help by supervising the children in the learning center room.

The above organizational patterns all indicate that teachers could work cooperatively to set up learning centers for their children. It is not necessary that teachers work cooperatively because there are many ways to use learning centers within the self-contained classroom. Some examples illustrating the physical set-up might include:

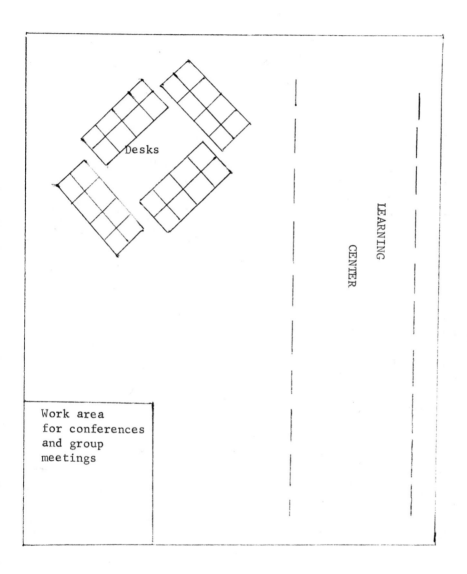

Desks

LEARNING

CENTER

Work area
for conferences
and group
meetings

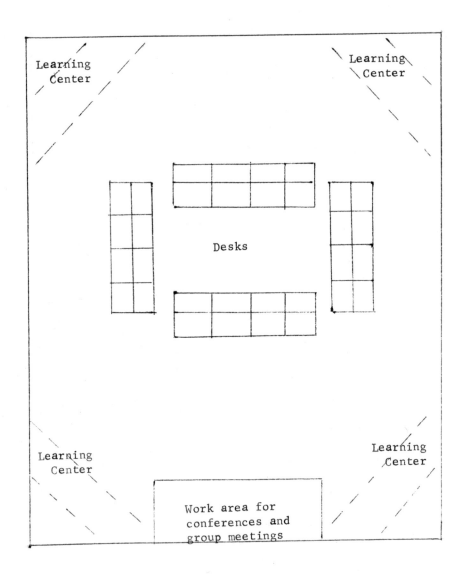

Learning
Center

Learning
Center

Desks

Learning
Center

Learning
Center

Work area for
conferences and
group meetings

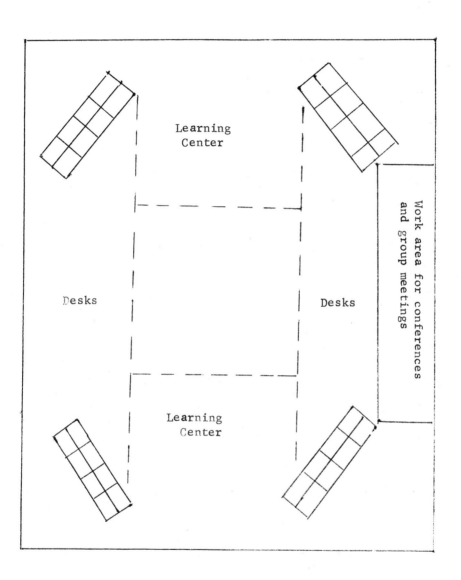

Learning
Center

Work area for conferences
and group meetings

Desks

Desks

Learning
Center

Other Organizational Patterns

The organizational patterns shown in the three diagrams illustrating learning centers within a self-contained classroom are by no means the only three types of patterns that can be used. There are many ways a classroom can be arranged to make the use of learning centers effective. The teacher is the best judge as to how his room could be arranged so that it would be comfortable for the students and the teacher and have the flexibility necessary to promote good individualized instruction.

After deciding about how the physical arrangement of the classroom can be utilized for the effective use of learning centers the teacher must decide which learning center or learning station approach he wants to use.

A teacher may adopt the learning center philosophy to help him individualize instruction on a very limited basis and during limited times or operate his class in a way that the children are spending much or most of their reading lesson working in learning stations in various centers.

An easy or sensible way to begin might be to select one of the reading groups and have a free time learning station during the reading lesson where children could work on reinforcing a new reading skill. If the teacher decides to expand into other areas within the field of reading, he could set up centers for such a purpose.

CHAPTER V

LIST I

SUGGESTED CAPTIONS FOR
LEARNING CENTERS TO MOTIVATE PUPILS

To plan, organize and construct effective learning centers, three specific lists will follow. List I may be used for selecting a caption. List II may provide ideas for teaching specific skills and List III may provide ideas regarding the developmental skills in the reading process. The sample learning stations following these lists will utilize materials from the three lists and will provide the teacher with a model for the development of learning centers.

List I

1. Ladder - How High Can You Climb?

2. Bell - Can You Ring the Bell?

3. Moon - Can You Land On the Moon?

4. Baseball - Can You Score a Homerun?

5. Football - Can You Score a Touchdown?

6. Basketball - Can You Sink a Basket?

7. Bee - Can You Be a Busy Bee?

8. Clown - Are You a Good Circus Clown?

9. Strong Man - How Strong Are You?

10. Bird - Will Your Birds Reach the Bird Sanctuary?

11. Scramble - Can You Unscramble These?

12. Drag Racing - Can You Get Across the Finish Line?

29

13. Fishing - Can You Catch a Fish?

14. Mouse - Can the Mouse Get to the Cheese?

15. Puzzle - Can You Put This Puzzle Together?

16. Guess - How Well Can You Guess?

17. Airplane Hangar - Can You Get the Airplane Into the Hangar?

18. Word Checkers - Who Can Play This Word Checker Game?

19. Treasure Hunt - Who Can Find the Biggest Treasure?

20. Hawaii - Who Can Get to Hawaii?

21. Steps - Who Can Get to the Roof?

22. Bus Terminal - Can You Get the Bus Into the Terminal?

23. Train - Can You Get the Train Into the Station?

24. Mystery Island - Who Can Escape From Mystery Island?

25. Blast Off - Who Will Be Able to Blast Off?

26. Authors - Are You a Good Author?

27. Farm - How Will You Get to the Farm?

28. City - How Will You Get to the City?

29. Disneyland - Who Can Get to Disneyland?

30. Word-O - Who Will Be the First to Call "Word O"?

31. Castle - Can You Cross the Moat to Get into the Castle?

32. Archery - Can You Hit the Bulls-Eye?

33. Ferris Wheel - How Many Turns Can You Get On the Ferris Wheel?

34. Roller Coaster - How Many Hills Can You Climb?

35. Merry-Go-Round - How Many Turns Can You Get?

36. Rodeo - Can You Break This Bronco?

37. Bull Fight - Can You Tame the Bull?

38. Cowboy or Cowgirl - Can You Ride Fast?

39. Pony Express - Who Can Get the Mail Delivered?

40. Telegraph - Can You Get Your Message Through?

41. Skiing - Can You Glide Without Falling?

42. Mountain Climber - Can You Climb This Mountain?

43. Astronaut - What Kind of Astronaut Are You?

44. Balloons - How Many Balloons Can You Blow Up?

45. Detective - Are You a Good Detective?

46. Horse Race - Can Your Horse Get to the Finish Line?

47. Lawyer - How Many Cases Can you Win?

48. Doctor - Are You a Good Doctor?

49. Mother - Are You a Good Mother?

50. Father - Are You a Good Father?

CHAPTER VI

LIST II

MODIFIED CAPTIONS AND QUESTIONS FOR
DEVELOPING SPECIFIC SKILLS IN READING

List II is designed to provide the teacher with some specific applications in learning centers with outcomes directed toward definite skills in reading. Other captions, some of which are derived from List I, are found in List II and serve as an additional resource for stimulating centers with clear-cut skills in mind.

List II

1. Vowel Sounds of "A" - Long and short - Do You Know the Long and Short Sounds of "A" in Words?

2. Word Bingo - Can You Recognize Words At Sight When They Are Pronounced For You?

3. Category Board - Can You Put the Animals, the Fruit, and the Plurals in The Right Category?

4. Word Opposites - Can You Clip the Clothespin With the Word Opposite Onto the Circle?

5. Contraction Board - Can You Match (using yarn) the Contractions With the Correct Words?

6. Try Your Hand at Writing - Can You Write a Story Using a Picture and the "Helping" Words Provided?

7. A Christmas Tree - Can You Find a Word On a Christmas Ball To Combine With One Already on the Tree to Make a Compound Word?

8. Help the Bees - Can You Make a Flower By Adding a Letter or a Blend to the Phoneme Provided?

9. Syllabication - Can You Use the Orange Strips to Divide the Words into Syllables?

10. Alphabetize - Can You Put the Words in the Box in Alphabetical Order?

11. Let's Play Categories - Can You Put the Words in Categories? Place them under the correct letter category, too.

12. Listening Center - Can You Hear the Long or Short Sound and Circle L or S?

13. Spelling Tree - Can You Spell the Word for the Picture on the Tree?

14. See How Brightly You Shine with Homonyms - Can You Use Your, You're, it's, its, etc. in Written Context?

15. Building Words - Can You Build a Compound Word?

16. Phonics Rules - How Well Do You Know Your Rules?

17. Find the Rhyme - Can You Find and Place on the Flannelboard the Words in the Can Which Rhyme?

18. Fishing for Antonyms - Can You Find the Opposites of Each?

19. Let's Follow Directions - Can You Listen and Construct the Game As I Tell You?

20. Clarence the Clown - Can You Group Your Spelling Words by Beginning Blends?

21. Who-oo is Wise? Can You Put the Phrases From the Stories Into Correct Sequence?

22. Descriptive Words - Can You Select Different Words to Describe the Picture?

23. Can You Solve a Case? - Can You Write Your Own Ending Solving the Case?

24. Build Super Power - Can You Expand Your Vocabulary by Building Compound Words?

25. My Own Story - Can You Build a Story Using the Beginning Paragraph and Ending Sentence Provided?

26. Who-oo Can List the Words? - Can You Separate the Group of Words Between the Guide Words Listed? Can you then put them in order?

27. Let's Use An Index! - Can You Answer the Questions Provided Using page 69 of the Yellow Pages?

28. What Do You Know? - Can You Recognize the "br" Words and Attach the Yarn to the Pictures?

29. Learning About Words - (a) Can You Listen, Follow Along, and Point to Pictures as I say Something About Each One?
         The man is tall.
         The boy is short.
(b) Can You Choose the Opposites and Put the Puzzle Cards Together?

(c) Can You Match Words That Are Opposites? (Back of card is color coded for checking)

(d) Can You Underline the Words in a Sentence Which are Opposites?
         Winter is <u>cold</u> but summer is <u>hot</u>.

30. Are the Vowel Sounds Alike? - Do the pictures and words have the same vowel sounds?

31. It's in the Bag! - Can You Select An Activity Envelope and Fill in the Blank on the Picture Card?
         Initial consonant <u>f</u> all
         Blend   <u>cr</u> eek
         Consonant digraph <u>ch</u> ur <u>ch</u>
         Vowel digraph   m <u>ai</u> d

32. Compound Words - Can You Take a Word From Each Pack and Put Them Into the Pockets As Compound Words?

33. Words in the Window - How Many Words Can You Say As You Slide the Cards Through the Cover Pack With a Window?

34. First Words First - If You Were Looking for these Words in the Dictionary Where Would You Find Them? The first fourth? Second fourth? Third fourth? Fourth fourth?

35. Touch Box - Can You Write a Short Description of How the Object in the Box Felt to You?

36. Expressions - Can You Describe in a List How You Think Each Persons Feels?

37. Vowel Bag Game - Can You Put the Word in the Correct Vowel Bag?

38. Sequence Board - Can You Look at the Pictures on the Board and Write a Story in Order About what is Happening?

39. Crazy Letters - Can You Unscramble the Spelling Words?

40. Climb the Giraffe's Neck - Can You Climb the Neck by Pronouncing each Word?

41. Definitions - Can You Match the Word With its Definition?

42. Look-at-Me Board - Can You Look at the Designs in Each Circle and Put One Just Like it From Those Provided on the Space Below It?

43. A Rhebus Story - Can You Find the Word on the Word Card and Cover the Picture in the Story With It?

44. Let's Play Match! - Can You Use Your Eyes to Play Match?

45. Picture Match - Can You Find Which are Alike and Which Are Different?

46. Unscramble the Pictures - Can You Listen to the Story and Put the Pictures in the Right Sequence?

47. Sentence Scramble - Can You Make a Good Sentence Choosing From the Scrambled Words?

CHAPTER VII

LIST III

READING SKILLS LIST

This is a suggested list of some of the skills which should be developed in a good reading program. The skills are organized developmentally according to various age levels. This skills list is not all inclusive. Within each level there are sequential skills which must be developed at different rates and times according to the individual needs of children. Good centers could be made up of stations which include skills selected from several different levels. An individual could be required to do one station within a center while another student who is more advanced would complete several stations. A teacher may find that within a given center there may be as many as four or five stations on different levels.

I. Ages Four to Six

A. Basic language skills - expression and recognition

    1. Recognizing name

    2. Knowing names of letters

    3. Knowing names of numerals

    4. Matching letters - lower to lower case, etc.

    5. Matching capital and lower case letters

    6. Matching numerals

7. Recognizing everyday words, such as: mother, father, boy, girl, dog, cat, etc.

8. Recognizing simple signs, such as: stop, go, green, red, slow, etc.

9. Matching pictures and words

B. Discrimination abilities

1. Auditory

a. Hearing difference between words of varying lengths

b. Listening for rhyming words

c. Listening for words with the same beginning sound

d. Listening for words with same ending sound

e. Listening for words with same medial sounds

f. Hearing the number of sounds in a word

g. Hearing differences in words

h. Listening to retell short two or three sentence story

i. Listening to difficult words or phrases until able to imitate them orally

j. Being able to cut out pictures that begin with the same sound

2. Visual

a. Using pointer or finger to follow left-right movement

b. Using picture clues or a rhebus

c. Matching colors

d. Matching objects

e. Matching pictures

f. Matching numbers

g. Matching letters

h. Matching words

i. Matching short sentences

j. Selecting word which is different

k. Selecting object which is different

l. Selecting numeral which is different

m. Selecting letter which is different

C. Motor abilities

1. Practicing tracing name

2. Practicing copying name

3. Practicing tracing letters

4. Practicing copying letters

5. Practicing tracing words

6. Practicing copying words

7. Practicing tracing designs

8. Practicing reproducing designs

D. Language abilities (Oral)

1. Talking about home and school

2. Reporting on interests

3. Sharing experiences

4. Retelling stories

5. Describing pictures

6. Telling original stories

7. Telling a new ending to a story

8. Finishing a sentence started by the teacher

E. Comprehension abilities

1. Remembering names of characters

2. Remembering main ideas

3. Knowing the ending or conclusion

4. Remembering the sequence of events

II. Ages Five to Seven

A. Vocabulary abilities

1. Having a basic sight vocabulary

2. Being able to recognize certain words in context such as: apple, Christmas, puppy, etc.

3. Recognizing words with capital and small letters

B. Word analysis abilities

1. Picture clues for story analysis

a. focusing attention on meaning

b. leading into a story

c. supplementary printed symbols

d. suggesting words to be used

e. providing clues to unknown words

2. Word-form clues

a. noticing length of words

b. seeing special features in words such as: tt, oo or final y, such as tail in "monke(y)"

c. noticing capital and small letters

d. noticing unique parts of words - look has two eyes in the middle

3. Phonics

a. recognizing single initial consonants and being able to make their sound

b. knowing single consonant sounds at end of words

c. knowing single consonant sounds at middle of words

d. beginning knowledge of vowel sounds

e. beginning knowledge of certain consonant blends and consonant digraphs, such as: sh, st, cl, etc.

4. Structural analysis

a. knowing inflectional endings such as ed, d, s, and ing

b. recognizing simple compound words, such as: someone, cowboy

c. knowing several word families

C. Comprehension abilities

1. Verifying statements

2. Placing events in sequential order

3. Following oral or printed directions

4. Recalling what has been read silently and orally

5. Identifying characters in the story and their good or bad points

D. Oral and silent reading abilities

1. Using correct pronunciation

2. Understanding simple punctuation marks

3. Reading silently without moving lips

4. Reading without moving head

III. Ages Six to Eight

A. Vocabulary abilities

1. Increasing basic sight vocabulary to include other words than in level two such as, thank, warm, these, etc.

2. Knowing many meanings of words

3. Knowing simple synonyms, such as: big-large

4. Knowing simple opposites, such as: big-small

5. Knowing simple homonyms, such as: know-no

B. Word analysis

1. Picture clues for story analysis

a. motivating the story

b. learning meanings of words

c. understanding the setting of story

d. helping see the characters of story more realistically

e. providing clues to unknown words

2. Word-form clues

a. noticing differences and likenesses in words

b. noticing unique parts of words particularly similarity in rhyming words as in sin, fin, win, etc.

3. Phonics

a. applying consonant sounds, blends and digraphs to beginning, middle, and end of words

b. knowing additional and more difficult word families such as, ow in show and ow in ow in cow, oi in oil, etc. (diphthongs)

c. knowing short vowel sounds

d. knowing long vowel sounds

e. understanding the use of y as a consonant and a vowel

f. knowing two sounds for c and g

g. understanding that one vowel in a word or syllable is usually short - (cut)

h. understanding that an e at the end of a word usually makes the preceding vowel long - (ride)

i. understanding that when two vowels are together in a word the first vowel is usually long - road - and the second is usually silent

j. understanding that when r, w and l follow a vowel the vowel is influenced such as in car, paw, ill

4. Structural analysis

a. recognizing more difficult compound words

b. knowing other word endings (suffixes), such as: ness, ly, ful, etc.

c. recognizing possessives

d. recognizing root words

C. Comprehension abilities

1. Dramatizing stories

2. Illustrating stories

3. Drawing conclusions

4. Predicting outcomes

5. Following more difficult printed directions

6. Proving an answer

7. Finding the main idea

8. Showing more detailed sequence of events

9. Using the Table of Contents

IV. Ages Seven to Nine

A. Vocabulary abilities

1. Knowing and using basic sight vocabulary words as Dolch Basic List

2. Knowing even more meanings of words

3. Having a more thorough knowledge of synonyms, homonyms and antonyms

4. Being able to select descriptive and figurative language

5. Being able to find the meaning of a word in the dictionary

B. Word analysis

1. Picture clues (The following skills are in more depth and proficiency than in previous levels)

   a. motivating story

   b. learning meanings of words

   c. understanding the setting of story

   d. helping see the characters of story more realistically

   e. providing clues to unknown words

2. Phonics (The following skills are in more depth and proficiency than in previous levels)

   a. applying consonant sounds, blends and digraphs to beginning, middle and end of words

   b. knowing different short vowel sounds

   c. knowing different long vowel sounds

   d. knowing silent letters such as wr and gn

43

e. understanding the use of the primary accent mark

f. knowing to accent the first syllable unless it is a prefix

3. Structural analysis abilities (The following skills are in more depth and proficiency than in previous level)

a. recognizing even more difficult compound words

b. knowing word endings such as s, es, est, d, etc.

c. knowing plurals by adding s, es, ies or by changing f to v and adding es

d. seeing similarities of sounds such as, x and cks (clocks-fox)

e. recognizing possessives

f. recognizing more difficult root words

g. recognizing and reading contractions

h. recognizing more difficult prefixes and suffixes

i. being able to hyphenate words into syllables by using simple syllabication rules

C. Comprehension abilities

1. Dramatizing stories in a creative fashion

2. Finding the main idea or ideas of a story

3. Using charts and diagrams to get understanding

4. Using the index - begin alphabetizing

5. Reading for pleasure

6. Reading to find specific answers to questions

7. Drawing logical conclusions

8. Being able to see relationships

9. Predicting outcomes

10. Writing a good ending to a story

11. Following more difficult printed directions

12. Distinguishing between reality and imaginary

V. Ages eight to ten

A. Vocabulary abilities

1. Getting meaning from context

2. Being able to find pronunciation and meanings of words from dictionary

3. Using new words in sentences to show meanings

4. Learning new words in content fields

5. Continuing and increasing knowledge of synonyms, homonyms and antonyms

6. Knowing many meanings for words

7. Using many meanings for words in different sentences

8. Substituting words for other words in the context

9. Using more descriptive words

10. Classifying words into categories

B. Word analysis

1. Phonics

a. reviewing all phonic skills previously taught at preceding levels in more depth

2. Structural analysis

a. pronouncing words not recognized as sight words

b. breaking words at the end of a line of writing

c. dividing into syllables between two consonants

d. knowing syllables are determined by vowel sounds heard

45

e. seeing that a single consonant between two vowels usually goes with the second vowel

f. knowing that consonant digraphs and consonant blends are not divided

g. knowing that certain endings constitute the final syllable such as ble, cle, gle, kle, etc.

h. knowing that prefixes and suffixes form separate syllables and have meanings

i. seeing that endings that form syllables are usually not accented

j. knowing that the first syllable is usually accented

k. knowing that the root word is often not divided

l. knowing the meaning of a syllable

m. knowing syllable phonics relating to closed and open syllables

n. knowing regular compound words as well as hyphenated compound words

3. Dictionary or glossary abilities

a. locating entries

b. alphabetizing according to first and second letters

c. using the pronunciation key

d. knowing diacritical markings

e. being knowledgeable about abbreviation

f. knowing how to use guide words

g. selecting the correct meaning

h. getting correct spelling

i. using illustrations to help with meanings

     j. knowing when to use the dictionary for finding correct syllables

C. <u>Comprehension abilities</u>

   1. Reading to discover cause and effect

      a. answering specific questions about a selection

      b. analyzing reasons for or causes of major events

      c. selecting facts to support main ideas

      d. verifying answers

   2. Reading for central thought

      a. reading a paragraph and giving the main idea

      b. choosing the best title

      c. finding the main idea of several ideas on a page

      d. finding the main idea of several pages or the whole selection

      e. making up a title for story

      f. making up sub-titles for parts of the story

      g. summarizing a page or several pages

      h. recognizing the topic sentence

   3. Reading for details

      a. answering specific questions

      b. finding certain information

      c. reproducing orally what happened

      d. remembering important facts

      e. remembering characters in story

   4. Reading for sequence of events

      a. arranging in order

b. telling what happened next

c. writing what will happen next

d. telling a different ending to a story

e. writing a different ending to a story

5. Reading to follow directions

a. carrying out written directions

b. being able to answer specific questions about directions

c. retelling directions in own words

d. writing directions in own words

6. Reading for outlining

a. knowing form for main and subordinate ideas

b. using central thought skills in helping to outline

c. being able to use outline to summarize orally or in written form

VI. Ages nine to eleven

A. Vocabulary abilities - reviewing abilities previously taught at other age levels and using in more depth

B. Phonics - reviewing abilities previously taught at other age levels and using in more depth

C. Dictionary or glossary abilities - reviewing abilities previously taught at other age levels and using in more depth

1. Learning abbreviated parts of speech, such as, v. - verb

2. Interpreting phonetic respellings

D. <u>Comprehension abilities</u> - reviewing abilities previously taught at other age levels and using in more depth

   1. Recognizing the function of parts of speech in context

   2. Interpreting figurative language

   3. Seeing shifts of meaning

   4. Distinguishing between fact and fiction

   5. Distinguishing between fact and opinion

   6. Anticipating meanings

   7. Seeing relationships between ideas

   8. Determining mood

   9. Determining author's theme

E. <u>Reading study abilities</u>

   1. Using the title

   2. Using Table of Contents

   3. Using the index

   4. Using the dictionary or glossary

   5. Using chapter headings

   6. Using unit headings

   7. Using illustrations and diagrams

   8. Using footnotes

   9. Using the encyclopedia

  10. Using graphs

  11. Using cross referencing

  12. Taking notes

  13. Being able to outline

14. Being able to summarize

15. Evaluating material for a purpose

16. Organizing reading material

17. Understanding different forms of writing

18. Understanding the card catalogue

19. Understanding guide letters on encyclopedias

20. Choosing correct reference material

VII. Ages ten to thirteen

A. Vocabulary abilities - reviewing abilities previously taught at other age levels and using in more depth

B. Phonics - reviewing abilities previously taught at other age levels and using in more depth

C. Dictionary or glossary skills - reviewing abilities previously taught at other age levels and using in more depth

D. Comprehension abilities - reviewing abilities previously taught at other age levels and using in more depth

1. Developing levels of abstractions

2. Anticipating meanings

3. Perceiving relationships between ideas

4. Evaluating relevancy of details to the main idea

5. Determining relationships between time and events

6. Interpreting humor

7. Interpreting characterizations

8. Predicting outcomes

E. Reading study abilities - reviewing abilities previously taught at other age levels and using in more depth

1. Being able to skim for a purpose

2. Reading for verification

3. Reading at different rates for different purposes

4. Reading critically

5. Using the preface

6. Using a bibliography

7. Using almanacs

8. Using maps and globes

9. Using the Atlas

10. Using the Dewey Decimal or Library of Congress system

11. Using indexes and Readers' Guides

12. Deciding on relevancy of ideas

13. Making more complicated outlines

14. Organizing information in the form of a graph

15. Organizing information in the form of a chart

16. Interpreting author's feelings

17. Identifying and writing a good topic sentence

18. Using a card catalogue

19. Reading for many purposes

CHAPTER VIII

SAMPLES OF LEARNING CENTERS AND STATIONS

Introduction

Earlier in this book it was mentioned that each of the preceding lists served a specific purpose in the development of learning stations within centers.

A few specific learning centers will be shown as a method for demonstrating the use of the three lists. Each station will be built around an idea from each list. The samples will specifically list the source of the idea so that the reader may check the source of each. This will provide a model for the teacher to follow so that hundreds of stations can be developed by multiple utilization of ideas within the three lists.

In order for the teacher to provide the very best centers for his students, he must state his objectives behaviorally in order to evaluate specifically what skills are to be accomplished through the use of the individual learning station. Each sample will contain behavioral objectives as a guide to the teacher.

Behavioral Objective - The child will be able to match the first ten capital and lower case letters.

Resource Lists - List I, #8 - Clown
List II, #20 - Clarence the Clown. Can you match the big and little letters? (variation)
List III, I-A-#5 - Matching capital and lower case letters

Materials - tag board
construction paper of different colors
unit card holder
sentence strips to cut

Diagram -

Are you a good circus clown?

Choose the matching big and little letters from the pocket.

Balloon   Answer

Pocket   Pocket

Directions - Choose the matching big and little letters from the pocket. (These are to be given orally by the teacher at this level.)

Evaluation - The child will check his own work by using the key in the answer pocket.

Note - The same or a similar format could be used to teach or review all letters of the alphabet.

Behavioral objective - The child will be able to say orally at least eight of twelve sight words.

Resource Lists - List I - #1 - Ladder (variation)
List II - #40 - Can You Climb the Giraffe's Neck? Can you climb the neck by pronouncing each word?
List III - II A - #1 - Developing basic sight vocabulary

Materials - construction paper
tagboard sentence strips
pins, tacks, magnets, or felt backing
flannel, chalk, or bulletin board

Diagram -

CAN

YOU

CLIMB

THE

GIRAFFE'S

NECK

Say each word.
Fasten it on his
neck until you
reach his head.

Directions - Say each word. Fasten it on the giraffe's neck until you reach his head. Use at least eight words. (Given orally by teacher.)

Evaluation - The child will check the work with a student helper or with the teacher. When a child knows all twelve sight words, he becomes a helper.

Note - After the twelve words are mastered, the teacher may use his knowledge of the children and add new sets of sight words using the above format.

Behavioral Objective - The child will be able to match ten sets of easy word opposites. (antonyms)

Resource Lists - List I - #13 - Fishing
List II - #18 - <u>Fishing for Opposites</u>
(Variation)
Can you find the opposite for each?
List III - III-A-#4 - Knowing simple opposites

Materials - Wooden easel
'Easel tray
Construction paper
Paper clips
Pole
String
Magnet
Desk

Diagram -

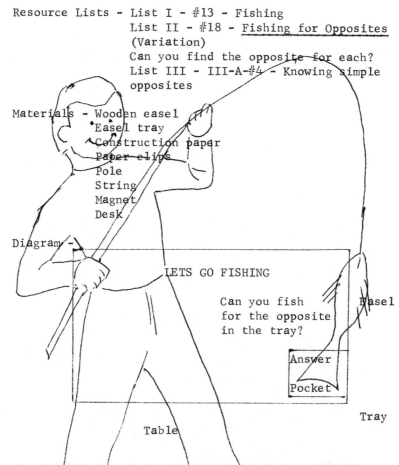

LETS GO FISHING

Can you fish
for the opposite
in the tray?

Easel

Answer
Pocket

Tray

Table

Directions - Can you fish for the opposites in the tray? Use a pole with an attached string and magnet. (Place a paper clip on each paper fish in the tray so that the magnet will attract them.)

Evaluation - The child will use the key in the answer pocket to compare the sets that he has made and placed on the desk in front of the easel.

Behavioral Objective - The child will be able to select
and use descriptive words in a story (oral or written)

Resource List - List I - #26 - Authors
                List II - #6 - Try Your Hand at Writing
                Can you write a story using this pic-
                ture and these words?
                List III - IV - A-#4 - Being able to
                select and use descriptive language

Materials - An exciting or appealing picture
           a small table or desk
           chalk ledge
           cardboard for mounting picture
           word box
           blank word cards (or 3X5 cards)

Diagram -

(Chalkboard)

ARE YOU A GOOD AUTHOR

Picture

Directions   Word Box

                                    Table

Writing Paper

Directions - Look at picture. Choose words from the word
box that help you describe the picture. Think of some descriptive words of your own to add to the word box. Using words
that you have thought of or chosen, write a short story about
the picture.

Evaluation - The child will submit his story to the
teacher or will share it with the other children.

Note - This station can be converted to an oral story
exercise by having children record their stories using a
cassette tape recorder.

Behavioral Objective - The child will write titles for several short stories.

Resource List - List I - #45 - Detective
    List II - #23 - Can You Solve a Case
    Can you write a good title?
    List III - V-C-#2e - Making titles for stories

Materials - wall or side of file cabinet, etc.
    construction paper for letters and packets
    three or four short stories
    desk
    slips of paper

Diagram -

ARE YOU A GOOD DETECTIVE?

Story #1	Story #2	Story #3	filing cabinet
Slips of paper		Answer slips	

Table

Directions - Read one or more of the stories. On the slip of paper provided write a good title for the story or stories which you read. Put your name on each slip of paper and put it into the slip box (or into your individual folder).

Evaluation - The teacher will collect and examine the answer slips of the children. Each child will be able to share a title with the group and tell why he chose that title.

Sample VI - Ages nine to eleven

Behavioral Objective - The child will be able to distinguish between fact and opinion.

Resource List - List I - #47 - Lawyer
List II - #21 - Who-oo is Wise?
(variation) Can you tell fact from opinion?
List III - VI-D-#5 - Distinguishing between fact and opinion

Materials - tape recorder (cassette or reel to reel)
cassette or tape
paper for responding
ear phones and jack (optional)
table
flannel board

Diagram -

LAWYER		Flannel Board
Who-oo is wise? Directions		
Example - The high tempera- ture yester- day was 82.°	Fact 1. 2.	Opinion 1. 2.	Example - It is going to rain because it is cloudy.
Tape Recorder	Paper	Answer Key	Table

Directions - Look at the display. Follow directions by listening to the recording of the ten statements of fact or opinion. On the numbered answer sheet provided, place f for fact or o for opinion. Use the answer key to check your answers. Extra wise lawyers may try to write at least three fact and three opinion statements of their own.

Evaluation - The student will check his own work for the first exercise. Extra wise lawyers will place their answers in their own folders or in an answer box which could be provided.

Behavioral Objective - The child will be able to find specific topics in the index.

Resource List - List I - #19 - Treasure Hunt
List II - #27 - Let's Use an Index
Can you answer the questions provided?
List III - VII - E-#11 - Using the index
(Reading-study abilities)

Materials - Yellow pages, World Almanac, etc.
Writing paper

Diagram -

TREASURE HUNT

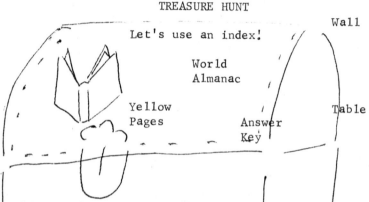

Let's use an index!

World
Almanac

Wall

Yellow
Pages

Answer
Key

Table

Directions - The child will be given a list of seven topics in each resource. On the answer sheet provided he will list the page where the topic can be found. The child will check his answers with those in the answer key provided.

Evaluation - The child will use the answer sheet to check his own work to see how well he can find specific topics in the index.

Note- The teacher may wish to extend this activity by requiring the student to answer questions in reference to topics being located.

<u>Sample VIII</u> - <u>A Sequential Learning Center</u> - <u>Ages seven to</u>
<u>thirteen</u>

The reader will find an example of a learning center containing three stations. The stations within the center are
related to one another and will reinforce a sequence of
dictionary skills.

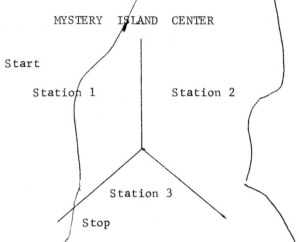

MYSTERY ISLAND CENTER

Start

Station 1   Station 2

Station 3

Stop

Age Level - Seven to thirteen - (depending on needs and
abilities of children)

Behavioral Objectives - (Station one) - The child will
be able to place a list of words in alphabetical order using
the first letter.

(Station two) - The child will be able to place a
list of words in alphabetical order using the first and second
letters.

(Station three) - The child will be able to place a
list of words in alphabetical order using as many letters as
needed to establish the correct order.

Resource Lists -
    Station One
    List I, #24 - Mystery Island
    List II - #10 - Alphabetizing
    List III - IV - C-#4

Station Two
Variation of same
Advanced alphabetizing
List III - V - B-#3b

Station Three
Variation of same
More advanced
List III - VI - C

Materials - Cardboard or pegboard for backing
            Pictures or drawings
            Construction paper
            Writing paper
            Desks or tables

Diagram -

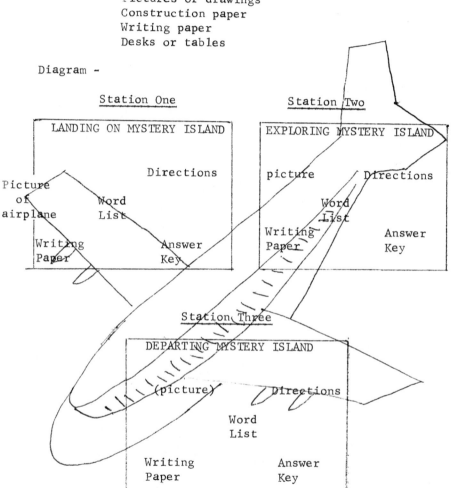

Station One

LANDING ON MYSTERY ISLAND

Directions

Picture
of
airplane

Word
List

Writing
Paper

Answer
Key

Station Two

EXPLORING MYSTERY ISLAND

picture   Directions

Word
List

Writing
Paper

Answer
Key

Station Three

DEPARTING MYSTERY ISLAND

(picture)   Directions

Word
List

Writing
Paper

Answer
Key

Directions - Select a list of words provided. Follow the directions for alphabetizing each as suggested. Compare your answers with the answer key at each station. Move on to the next station. When you have completed station three you may leave Mystery Island.

Evaluation - The child must complete correctly all three alphabetical listings. (Station three could have an additional list combining the three levels of skills. The child who completes this list leaves by superjet.)

CHAPTER IX

GUIDELINES IN THE EVALUATIVE PROCESS

The aspect of evaluation is a very basic one in using learning stations in the classroom. First, the teacher must have a good grasp of sequential skills in order to guide and to evaluate teaching and learning. The authors have, therefore, provided a sequential list of skills in reading which the teacher may use to elaborate or to sub-divide according to needs of children.

Secondly, as another aid to the teacher, this text provides information about and examples of behavioral objectives which can be used to evaluate progress or to measure progress. These two devices are provided in order to give the teacher concrete help in planning and in evaluation.

Further, day-to-day evaluation of each child's progress is basic to any individualized approach to learning.

Evaluating student progress within the learning center approach may include three different types:

1. Teacher-student conference
2. Student-student conference
3. Student-self evaluation

Teacher-Student

Probably the best and most meaningful evaluation that can go on is for the classroom teacher and the student to have periodic conferences in relation to the learning stations.

Students could keep folders containing samples of work completed, as well as, checklists on which they have recorded completed learning stations. By bringing such information to the classroom teacher during the individual teacher-student conference the teacher gains diagnostic information which assists in planning future individualized instruction.

Student-Student

Children who are particularly skillful in adapting to learning stations could be used as group leaders. In a group leader-student conference the group leader could check many of the items that the teacher would normally check. He could report such findings to the classroom teacher or guide the students who may be having difficulty so that when the teacher-pupil conference is held it would be greatly facilitated.

Student Self-evaluation

The role of the classroom teacher and that of the group-leader would constantly emphasize the importance to each student of evaluating himself and as a consequence, through such self-evaluation the individual conferences with the teacher could be most productive.

CHAPTER X

GENERAL CONSIDERATIONS AND CONCLUDING STATEMENT

The learning center approach and the use of learning stations within such an approach is not the answer to all questions on individualized learning. There are some criticisms of the total use of such an approach. For one thing there is not yet a solid pool of research which proves or disproves that learning centers are highly productive in the educational setting. A second criticism seems to be that certain children do not have the self-discipline or maturity to operate well in independent self-directed activities. A third criticism is that too much work is involved on the teachers part and a fourth is that evaluation or grading of learning stations is most difficult.

The authors of this text feel that they have addressed themselves to helping to solve the problems stated above. The use of this text should help the teacher diminish the work load. The fact that a few children lack the self-discipline or maturity to participate in such activities should not keep educators from providing such experience for other children, as well as, to help the children who lack the skills to participate by becoming more involved in independent learning activities. In fact, as will be pointed out, one of the advantages of learning centers is that they give practice in self-discipline. As to waiting for research to prove that the learning centers approach is beneficial to learning tasks - one might wait for years before adopting the use of this individualized procedure which many thousands of teachers are finding appropriate to the teaching-learning process. Using the behavioral approach as has been spelled out in this text as well as following the suggestions in the previous section should help make evaluation of learning centers less of a burden.

There are advantages to using Learning Centers or Learning Stations with Learning Centers. Such advantages for the teacher include:

1. Individualizing instruction and learning
2. Encouraging children to work at their own rate
3. Working in small groups
4. Taking pressure off of children
5. Developing responsibility
6. Increasing motivation to learn
7. Giving practice in self-discipline

Using learning centers to develop skills will take time and will require slow and orderly introduction of students and even teachers to the concept. Teachers and children must proceed at their own rates. They must develop skills of evaluation, security in the use of media, flexibility in devising centers, revised grading systems, and an openness about the teaching and learning atmosphere that fosters greater independence of thought and movement on everyone's part.